The Brutal Truth About Relationships

The Brutal Truth About Relationships

SYLVIE QUINN

Thought Catalog Books
Brooklyn, NY

THOUGHT CATALOG BOOKS

Copyright © 2016 by The Thought & Expression Co.

All rights reserved. Published by Thought Catalog Books, a division of The Thought & Expression Co., Williamsburg, Brooklyn. Founded in 2010, Thought Catalog is a website and imprint dedicated to your ideas and stories. We publish fiction and non-fiction from emerging and established writers across all genres. For general information and submissions: manuscripts@thoughtcatalog.com.

First edition, 2016

ISBN 978-1530125050

10 9 8 7 6 5 4 3 2 1

Cover photography by © Krista Mangulsone

Contents

1. 10 Brutally Honest Reasons Why Long-Term Couples Actually Stay Together — 1
2. 10 Ways You're Making Your Relationship Harder Than It Has To Be — 7
3. 10 Reasons You Need To Stop Bitching About Your Partner's Ex(es) Right This Second — 13
4. 25 Beautifully Banal Ways True Love Manifests Day-To-Day — 19
5. 20 Relationship Hiccups Even The Happiest Couples Experience — 23
6. 23 Relationship Hang-Ups You Need To Get Over Right Now If You Want Lasting Love — 27
7. 23 Weird But Endearing Sex Moments All Healthy Couples Eventually Experience — 31
8. You Have To Evolve Together, Or Go Your Separate Ways — 35
9. 25 Tiny Ways The Love Of Your Life Is Bound To Drive You Crazy (Because That's Just Life) — 39
10. 21 Brutal Relationship Truths Healthy Couples Accept (Because They Know They Have To) — 43
11. 50 'What Ifs' Even The Most Compatible Couples Need To Consider Before Settling Down Together Forever — 47
12. Cute Or Creepy? 17 Adorably Weird Things Healthy Couples Secretly Do Together — 53
13. 10 Things That Stress You Out In A New Relationship (That You Get To Stop Caring About Six Months Later) — 57
14. 10 Tips On How To Live With Someone For The Rest Of Your Life Without Going Fucking Crazy — 63
15. 19 Signs Your Relationship Is (Pretty Much) Stronger Than The Green Monster — 69

16.	9 Ways Men Push The Boundaries Of Fidelity Without Technically Cheating (The Way They See It)	73
17.	23 Unromantic Realities You Have To Accept If You Want Lasting Love	79
18.	10 Weird Things That Happen During Sex When You're Monogamous For Long Enough	83
19.	21 Unpleasant Truths Healthy Couples Are Better Off Never Thinking About	89
20.	19 Signs Your Broken Relationship Is Totally Worth Saving	93
21.	Read This If You're Feeling Betrayed By Your Boyfriend Or Girlfriend	97
22.	Read This If You're Having Doubts About Your Relationship	101

1

10 Brutally Honest Reasons Why Long-Term Couples Actually Stay Together

1. They're terrified of breaking up—from a logistical standpoint.

At a certain point in a relationship—once you've moved in together and your lives, including your schedules and finances, are nearly 100% intertwined—the prospect of splitting up becomes intimidatingly tedious. Breaking up might seem like a great idea in the aftermath of a nasty fight, but only until you remember what a raging headache it would be to separate from a practical standpoint. It's not the hypothetical emotional anguish of heartbreak that keeps people together, necessarily. Sometimes, it's fear of the logistical nightmare associated with dividing two intricately connected lives. Moving out, separating accounts, and explaining what went down to family and friends are all highly unpleasant tasks. As humans, we're programmed to choose the path of least resistance, so we stay together because it's just simpler sometimes.

2. They know too many intimate details about each other.

Over time, you acquire encyclopedic knowledge of the person you're dating. Eventually, you know most of your significant other's passwords, their social security number, and their answers to the typical security questions. You also know every embarrassing detail from their past, every shortcoming, and every vulnerability. No one wants an enemy armed with that much intel, so couples that know each other inside and out are incentivized to figure their shit out rather than split, which would mean releasing a scary knowledgable potential adversary out into the world. We all have a vested interest in keeping well-informed parties close.

3. They possess vast archives of potential blackmail material.

Nowadays, sex tapes aren't just the territory of the Kardashians and fame hungry Z-list celebrities. It's easy for couples to get drunk, prop an iphone up at an angle, hit record, and film a little DIY porno. Since we're all recording such a staggering percentage of our mundane lives, it's also easy to lose track of video content. Is that three-minute oral sex vid living on your hard drive or theirs? How about the footage of that 10-minute BDSM experiment gone wrong? And what about all those sexts? In some of those sexy shots, you even included your face as a demonstration of trust and faith in the relationship. As much as you'd like to believe that your partner of several years would never *ever* have the heart or the audacity to blackmail you, can you really be so sure???

4. They're all over each other's social media accounts.

Your significant other is probably an integral part of your online history. They're at the center of your social feeds because everyone loves an adorable shot of a happy couple so you lean on those for "likes" when you need to feel better about life. If you were to part ways, you'd either have to leave that evidence of your past relationship sitting around to haunt you every time you scroll through your social feeds, or go back and untag/delete your former boo from every single post they're featured in. Neither option is all that appealing. Why not just stick it out instead?

5. The very idea of dipping back into the dating pool exhausts them.

Whenever you're out at a bar or a restaurant, you pinpoint the couples in the early stages of dating within seconds of overhearing their stilted conversations. Listening to all of that awkward, boring small talk makes you supremely grateful to be well past the point of feigning interest in the details of your date's daily commute and local weather patterns. Reentering the world of singles might be fun for a minute, but the thrill of sleeping around would wear off at some point, and building actual intimacy from square requires a serious amount of work. Sigh.

6. They already have each other's bodies figured out.

The process of getting to know someone's body and learning how to pleasure them most effectively is draining, as it requires a good deal of communication, cooperation, and vulnerability from both parties. Plus, it's not easy to find someone you can love and respect whom you also want to fuck regularly. There are so many factors that play into sexual chemistry. So if you and your current lover are compatible in the sack, repairing whatever's wrong between you often seems like a more attractive option than launching a search for yet another needle in the haystack of people-you-want-to-hang-out-with-and-also-bang.

7. They're part of each other's extended families.

Throughout years of dating, you inevitably start to think of your partner's family as an extension of your own even if you're not engaged or married. You celebrate holidays together and your significant other's siblings' and parents' birthdays are ingrained in your memory. After a certain point, breaking up means leaving your partner *and* their family. The more people you have to leave behind, the more traumatic the potential shake-up. No thanks.

8. They don't want to trash all the stuff they've given each other.

Between Valentine's Day, anniversaries, and birthdays, you've probably gifted your significant other with quite a few nice pieces of jewelry or expensive electronics or cheap but meaningful knickknacks. Separating would mean using or wearing said things at the risk of triggering unwanted past memories, or giving them up all together. It's tough to part with nice stuff, but you don't have to if you can find some way to keep the relationship in tact.

9. They have all the same friends.

Don't be fooled into thinking it's possible for anyone to be the Sweden of their social circle by staying neutral and friendly with both members of a relationship post breakup. It's not how it works. Everyone has to choose a side, and that sucks. None of your friends want to be forced into the Sophie's Choice position of aligning with either you or your significant other. Understanding this, a lot of people in long-term relationships would rather go home to someone they low-key hate for a while than be part of the divisive Berlin Wall duo responsible for messing up monthly game night.

10. They love the fuck out of each other.

The thing about relationships is that they tend to grow stronger with time all on their own. Moments are constantly transforming into shared memories, good and bad. Nothing can stop the timeline of your existence as a couple from getting longer, day after day, or the roots of your bond from growing deeper minute by minute (unless of course you split). Things don't always have to be going swimmingly for your relationship to strengthen. You are a unit. You are best friends.

And you love the fuck out of each other—most of the time, at least.

2

10 Ways You're Making Your Relationship Harder Than It Has To Be

1. You're assuming that true love should be easy.

When you fall in love, even the most mundane aspects of life suddenly take on new meaning. As much as you enjoy watching your favorite movie, it's doubly awesome to watch it alongside your significant other so you can experience the cinematic pleasure from their perspective too. But while living day-today with someone you love can be incredibly fulfilling, it isn't easy—not even for the happiest couples. There will be days when you wake up quasi-hating each other, stretches of time when your moods fall out of sync and you can't seem to enjoy each other's company *at all*, and weeks when everything seems to be going wrong for no reason. Love isn't some magical force that protects you from Life's shit. You have to work hard to steer through all the crap if you want to stay together. True love takes teamwork, and it's hard AF.

2. You're a little *too* truthful with each other.

I hate to burst anyone's romantic bubble, but total transparency doesn't facilitate lasting love. You don't have to be totally honest with someone to build a foundation of trust. Sometimes, fibbing or omitting the truth is the decent thing to do. Your partner will *need* you to lie to them sometimes—to protect them from the reality that you woke up in the middle of the night fantasizing about another man or woman, or that they don't actually look amazing in that new outfit you can sense they feel so confident rocking. There are times when a little white lie can go a long way in sparing a person pain and heartache. As long as you're well-intentioned, skirting the truth isn't always such a bad thing to do.

3. You're comparing your relationship to others'.

It's tempting—natural, even—to draw comparisons. With everyone broadcasting the highlights of their lives over social media and using ridiculous hashtags (e.g. #proudwife #solucky #loveourlife) to accentuate their boastful posts, it's virtually impossible not to feel like you're falling short in the happiness department sometimes. You want to be sure that you're in a "good relationship"—that you're not less happy than you *should* be. But the fact is that social media isn't an accurate portrayal of anyone's life. You know this because you curate your own feed to reflect your best self, featuring only the most glamorous, loving moments, all of which are filtered. With or without social media, the only two people who know what's going on in a relationship are the people who are actually in it. It's impossible to know what other couples' lives are really like, so measuring your relative happiness against theirs is a laughably futile exercise.

4. You're looking at fighting as a problem rather than a chance to learn.

Passion is awesome when it's directed towards adoring the person you love, but when something goes wrong and your passionate feelings are suddenly coupled with acute anger, things can get nasty fast. When you know someone intimately, you have a lot of power to hurt that individual. At your weakest points, you will use that power recklessly. You will become the worst version of yourself, saying and doing things so out of character that your own behavior disgusts you in real time. You won't stop—until you do. Every storm eventually passes, and when it does, it leaves an opportunity to learn in its wake. If you take something positive away from every battle, thereby seizing the chance it presents to do better, you will be far less likely to repeat the same mistakes. Fighting isn't a sign of your impending downfall as a couple. It's just part of the deal, really.

5. You're not apologizing often enough.

The simple act of saying "sorry" regularly is critical. Why? Because you're going to make *a lot* of mistakes as time goes by—some purely by accident, others out of complete idiocy, and still others because your inner jerk decides to shine through. Remember, you're human. You'll step on your partner's already sore pinky toe at the suckiest time, you'll forget to pick up the dry cleaning one night as you promised you would, or you'll say something appallingly insensitive just to fuck with the person you love. Hopefully, you'll regret every mistake you make, large and small. But *feeling* bad isn't enough. You have to convey your remorse clearly every single time. If you want to grow as a couple, after all, you have to commit to personal growth, which requires shelving your ego and admitting when you're in the wrong.

6. You're dwelling on the past.

Healthy relationships are built on forgiveness and acceptance. Your significant other is an accumulation of everything they've experienced to date, so you have to accept every piece of their past, including those relationships with exes you'd rather not acknowledge and those ridiculously misguided things they did as a young adult. If either person is consumed by frustration over things that occurred in the other's past, contempt will eat away at the relationship until its totally dead. You *have* to let go—not just in the beginning, when you first learn the details of your partner's history, but throughout the relationship. As time goes by and you accumulate shared experiences—some good, some bad—you'll have to practice forgiveness and plow ahead without harping on the problems you once faced. The art of moving on requires compassion and patience, and it's crucial to long-term contentment.

7. You're fixating on the future.

It's always a good idea to set goals as a couple and to work towards meeting them together. Tackling a new exercise regimen seems a lot more like a fun game and less like an impossibly gargantuan, unpleasant task when you do it with someone you love. So does saving up to buy a new car, or speculating about what life would look like with kids in the equation. But if all you can think about is what you want from your future together, you'll end up devoting too much mental energy to what might be instead of what *is*. You have to be careful not to dream at the cost of appreciating the present.

8. You're interpreting every relationship doubt as a bad omen.

Only a fool is 100 percent certain of anything. No matter how deeply devoted you are to your boyfriend or girlfriend, you're destined to doubt the strength of your bond occasionally. You will question whether or not you're with the right person, and wonder if you'll be able to make it long-term. You will speculate about what life would look like, had you made different romantic choices. There's no shame in entertaining relationship uncertainty. Doubt creeps in when you least expect it, and it can feel like a serious betrayal of the person you love. But examining your life as an individual and as part of a couple is an entirely healthy pursuit. It certainly doesn't mean that you weren't meant to be together, or that you love your partner any less.

9. You're afraid of change.

Change can be terrifying, but it's also inevitable. Over time, circumstances beyond your control will force you to move or to switch careers or to adopt a new diet. You and your partner are both likely to change in ways you can't predict at this very moment. You'll pick up new hobbies and make new friends. One of you might join a different political party, or suddenly develop an interest in religion. People aren't static. They're fluid. You can't shy away from change, even if it means deviating from the path that led you to each other. Instead, you have to find a way to evolve together.

10. You're setting outlandish expectations.

Falling in love isn't the answer to everything. Your relationship, even at its best, won't necessarily make you feel whole, or happy. You will still have to answer to yourself every day, and figure out how to lead a fulfilling life. You have to figure your own shit out, so to speak—and even when you have a supportive, loving partner at your side, it's tough. Don't expect love to fix your life. When you set crazy expectations like that, you set yourself up to be crazy disappointed. There's no such thing as a one-way ticket to Happily Ever After.

3

10 Reasons You Need To Stop Bitching About Your Partner's Ex(es) Right This Second

1. You don't get unconditional, lasting love without forgiveness.

The path to Happily Ever After is paved in acceptance and forgiveness—and not the piecemeal kind. If you want a healthy long-term relationship, you can't pick and choose which pieces of your partner's past to accept while dismissing others (like that one particularly loathsome cunt they almost proposed to in college) as repugnant or unmentionable. Instead, you have to figure out how to accept the entire complicated package that is your significant other, including every single difficult-to-stomach romantic ~~mistake~~ choice they've ever made.

2. The fact that your significant other once dated someone

you have a hard time not hating doesn't constitute a character "con."

Maybe certain things about some of your partner's exes—what they do for a living, how they dress, or the fact that they're vegan—make you want to swallow a pound of sharp pins and chase it with a giant glass of bleach. Truth is, your partner is no less worthy of love and respect just because they dated someone with unfortunate taste in food, or footwear. (It's not like they're still *with* any of those weirdos anyway.)

3. You probably don't even really know any of your partner's exes.

You can cyberstalk all you want and demand answers to all the prying questions you can conceive as you tumble down the rabbit hole of wondering-what-your-lover's-life-was-like-with-that-other-person-whose-name-you-dare-not-speak-aloud, but unless you happen to know your partner's exes personally, all the information you gather amounts to a shoddy, super low pixelated picture of an individual.

4. It's idiotic to hate someone you don't know.

Why bother devoting any time or energy to despising a person you don't even know? It sounds absolutely ridiculous. Because it is! You're above that kind of spite—starting *now*.

5. Harboring resentment is actually bad for your health.

Consider how good it feels to entertain kind thoughts, and, conversely, how horrible it feels to wallow in negativity. Bitterness isn't healthy for your mind or body, so why let your imagination concoct angry narratives centering people your partner dated before you, the obvious upgrade to all priors, entered the picture?

6. Envy is totally unbecoming.

If preserving your mental and physical health isn't incentive enough to stop you from resorting to ex-loathing, consider the fact that fixating on your partner's past romantic "mistakes" is downright ugly. Yes, a little reciprocal jealousy can be beneficial to a relationship. But obsessing over your partner's exes is a sign of acute jealousy rooted in insecurity, which is entirely unattractive. On the other hand, self-confidence is undoubtedly sexy.

7. Remember, you have exes too.

Trust me, your partner doesn't enjoy thinking about you spooning—let alone fucking—anyone else. It's just as easy for them to fall into the vortex of ex-resentment. On the upside of such toxicity, the reality is that you're in the exact same boat. You can either let your shared concerns tear you apart, or tackle any unwanted *ew* moments as a couple, growing closer as you help each other overcome your true feelings.

8. Whether you like it or not, your significant other is an accumulation of ALL their life experiences, including times spent with all those irksome exes.

Each of us is on an ongoing journey of personal growth comprised of everything that ever happens to us. Insulting your partner's exes is tantamount to rejecting tiny portions of their personal history—and, by extension, who they are as a person today as a result—which is pretty fucking rude if you think about it.

9. You're the person chosen by the most evolved version of your boyfriend or girlfriend.

The person your partner is today is more mature, well educated, and awesomer than the person they were when they chose to date all those other people before you. So think of yourself as an upgrade—half of the most state-of-the art coupledom either of you has ever been a part of. All those other dalliances amount to nothing compared to the long stretch of future happiness that looms before you two highly evolved lovers.

10. If you feed it, contempt will actually kill your relationship.

Nurturing disdain for any aspect of your partner, including their past romantic escapades, is like releasing a slow-moving but deadly flesh-eating disease in the petri dish encasing your bond. Maybe you cringe at the thought of your boyfriend or girlfriend's involvement with one of their exes in particular, no matter how hard you try to reframe your attitude. You can't believe that someone *you're* with ever connected to someone you so revile. Either find it in your heart to get over it, or move on. Because scornful thinking is dangerous. It inevitably oozes into every other area of your life as a couple, tainting all the good stuff that brought you together in the first place.

4

25 Beautifully Banal Ways True Love Manifests Day-To-Day

1. Love is using each other's razors or deodorant because it makes you feel closer in some weird way you can't quite explain.

2. It's also laughing over how bad your farts stink, and sometimes arguing feverishly over whose farts stink more.

3. It's calling your significant other out for being an asshole, or letting them slide for their asshole behavior because they had a no-good, horrible, very bad day and they need a permission slip to be a dick temporarily.

4. It's negotiating constantly over ridiculous matters, and making silly bargains. For instance, "I'll consent to those questionable throw pillows *if and only if* you agree to those kitchen towels I like."

5. It's debating which TV show you should watch together next, and claiming the right to view certain programs alone so you can't be accused of TV-cheating later.

6. It's giving your significant other a two-minute back rub before falling asleep even if you're exhausted simply because they ask you to (and you know they're good for the massage credit).

7. It's establishing life-enhancing household rules like No Phones At The Dinner Table Ever. And punishing each other appropriately on the occasions either of you violates an agreed upon stipulation.

8. It's looking into each other's eyes whenever possible, understanding that eye contact is generally more powerful than anything that comes out of either of your mouths.

9. It's spending ten minutes neither of you has lazing about in bed some mornings after the alarm rings before you pick up your phones and dive into the day ahead.

10. It's telling your significant other that they look sexy before they even ask for your opinion on the days you sense they could use the ego boost.

11. It's remembering when your boyfriend or girlfriend has an important meeting and offering a canned but meaningful "good luck" as they head out the door.

12. Then remembering to text them an appropriately uplifting, emoji-ridden message right before that meeting occurs.

13. And preparing to support them no matter the outcome of that big important meeting because you've committed to being there whatever the fuck happens.

14. It's preemptively doing tiny little things to make each other happy, like putting the laundry in the dryer even if you didn't start the wash, or tidying up the closet even if you didn't create that hideous mess.

15. It's doing the dishes when it's not your turn because you can sense that your partner might benefit from heading directly to the couch right after dinner.

16. It's saying "thank you" for every little thing your partner does for you. And sometimes, saying it for no apparent reason, without prompting, because you truly feel grateful for the life you've built together.

17. It's sighing slash smiling over the fact that your partner failed, yet again, to put the toothpaste or the salt or the remote control back in its designated place after using it—not because they didn't think to do so, but because they know exactly how to push your buttons.

18. It's letting your boyfriend or girlfriend use you as an excuse to get out of something they don't want to do. "Sorry, can't make it to dinner. [Insert s/o's name] is sick with the flu. Again."

19. It's entertaining your partner's friends when they pop by unexpectedly, even when hosting is the last thing in the world you feel like doing.

20. It's taking a genuine interest in each other's hobbies—reading up about motorcycles or stamp collecting or football or whatever else tickles your significant other—just so you can ask each other questions that demonstrate you care enough to research shit you don't really care about.

21. It's making up words so you can speak in your very own couple's code.

22. It's encouraging each other to make smart eating choices and to exercise regularly because teamwork makes maintaining healthy habits so much simpler.

23. It's also making bad choices together—like gong for ice cream on a full stomach or finishing a second or third bottle of wine on a weeknight—for the hell of it because indulging as a twosome is doubly satisfying.

24. It's saying "I love you" at seemingly random moments, and then casually returning to whatever else you were just doing.

25. It's reminding each other that you're lucky to be together—and that you can't imagine life without the option to collapse into each other's arms whenever.

5

20 Relationship Hiccups Even The Happiest Couples Experience

1. When one person asks, "Why do you love me?" and the other struggles to answer readily, or provides a canned reply instead of saying something sincere.

2. When your significant other says something so deeply offensive, you have to wonder whether they like—let alone *love*—you enough to justify staying together.

3. When you realize that the lust you once felt during the early stages of dating isn't quite there anymore, and even though something more remarkable and lasting has taken its place, you ache to resurrect the blind, obsessive passion that first drew you to each other. Knowing that you can't definitely sucks.

4. When you wake up from an awesomely sexy dream starring someone other than your boyfriend or girlfriend and the awareness that you can't make your fantasy a reality because you're in an exclusive relationship brings you down, at least until you drink your morning coffee.

5. When you're thinking about a lifetime of fidelity with the person you adore, and you just can't shake the skeptical, *how-the-fuck-do-couples-actually-do-it?* thoughts from tainting your heart.

6. When something about your partner's past is revealed that makes you cringe out of disdain for who they once were, or what they once stood for.

7. When accepting the fact that your partner is a living, breathing accumulation of every choice they've ever made—including the decision to fuck all those other people (before you saved them)—proves more difficult than you wish.

8. When one person is caught lying about even the most innocuous thing and that minor fib inevitably undermines their credibility, at least temporarily.

9. When you fail to comfort your partner in the aftermath of a devastating life event or a typical bad day, and then someone else—a friend, a sibling, or a parent—steps in and proves way more helpful, kind of compromising your position as Most Important Person in your lover's life.

10. When a tough period or a nasty fight inspires someone to wonder, out loud, what life would look like if they'd never broken up with their ex.

11. When you both have to acknowledge that you'd probably benefit from an afternoon apart, doing separate things, even though you don't get all that much time together.

12. When jealousy prevents you from being genuinely happy for your significant other, or makes you act like an asshole rather than being supportive.

13. When one person behaves in a mind-blowing way, forcing you to question how well you really know each other.

14. When someone's new friend or hobby totally turns the other off, and you both start to doubt how much you have in common.

15. When the idea of having kids leads you to draft a mental checklist of the traits you hope your baby does (and *doesn't*) inherit from your significant other.

16. When you dare to "go there"—to that place you know better than to visit because doing so will lead to the worst kind of hurt—and then quickly regret it, but the damage is already done.

17. When an apology rings false, exacerbating an already prickly situation.

18. When someone secretly isn't all that amped for a special occasion or a date night that's been planned forever so they try to feign excitement but it's frustratingly obvious that they're not in the mood or as present as they should be.

19. When you realize that maybe you're the one who's behavior is toxic to the relationship and you're not quite sure how to make things better.

20. When you think about what exactly keeps you together and the truth isn't all that romantic. The glue might just be something banal, like shared stubbornness, or a mutual appreciation for Game of Thrones and a consistent desire to go to bed early. And yet, it works.

6

23 Relationship Hang-Ups You Need To Get Over Right Now If You Want Lasting Love

1. You'll never be able to read your significant other's mind. So you'll never be able to confirm whether they're being truthful at any given time.

2. That means you'll have to rely on your instincts *a lot*. And sometimes your gut will be flat-out wrong.

3. Other times, your gut will be on point, but you'll be fooled into thinking otherwise by your mostly well-meaning but sometimes crafty partner.

4. The longer you stay together, the better positioned you'll be to manipulate each other simply because knowledge is power.

5. When you find yourself exploiting your vast knowledge of your partner to get what you want, you'll probably feel a little bit guilty, but not quite bad enough to stop.

6. You will both say a lot of things you don't really mean just to shut each other up. There'll be plenty of false positives (*You really are always right, sweetie!*), and false negatives (*I hate your mother fucking guts!*).

7. You'll even offer half-true assertions for the hell of it sometimes (*You give the best blowjobs of anyone I've ever been with! You're the sexiest person I've ever dated! I absolutely adore hanging out with your family!*), because it seems like the decent thing to do.

8. Your partner will not always want to have sex with you, even when they claim to. Alternatively, they might say that your hot naked body put them in the mood when a secret fantasy did the trick instead.

9. You will both inevitably meet other people whom you know, instinctively, you could also probably love. So you will have to choose each other over and over and over again. Or move on.

10. You'll both regularly encounter other people you'll want to sleep with, too. So you'll both have to choose to honor whatever boundaries you've established as a couple again and again and again. Or risk stepping outside the bounds of commitment.

11. It will be a joint struggle to resist all the temptations you face over the years. And you may or may not ever know whether you're both successful.

12. You'll have to support your partner through some rough times when providing reassurance and propping another person up is the last thing you're in the mood to do.

13. You'll have to make your partner feel sexually attractive even when you kind of hate what they're wearing, and make them feel loved even on the days when you more than kind of resent them.

14. Sometimes, you won't be able to cheer each other up no matter how hard you try. Love won't solve all your problems because it's not a magic fix. It's a transcendent bond with tremendous rewards that sometimes *causes* problems.

15. You will both waste time pining over matters that don't actually matter simply because you're human and that's life.

16. There will be periods when your imaginations run wild and you can't stop your own minds from opening the floodgates of paranoia and doubt.

17. Your brains and hearts will sometimes urge you to get jealous when there's absolutely no reason to worry about anything.

18. At other times, you'll fail to be suspicious when you absolutely should be.

19. Your partner will lie to you—about little things (like what they *really* think about your new jeans), and bigger things (like exactly what went down at the strip club that one night).

20. No matter how crazy it sounds, you probably *need* them to lie to you on occasion, because total transparency is pretty damn impossible to live by. The health of your relationship and your personal sanity will most likely depend on many well-intentioned fabrications.

21. Over time, you will say a lot of truthful and untruthful nasty things to each other—because hurting the person you adore, again and again, is absolutely inevitable.

22. Even after years, you'll overlook things about your significant other—how they're really feeling, what they actually want for dinner, or why they're disproportionately upset about something—because not even the most attentive people are perfect, so no couple can be.

23. No matter how strong your bond is, you'll never know the love of your life entirely because no one can know 100 percent of anyone. And that's okay.

7

23 Weird But Endearing Sex Moments All Healthy Couples Eventually Experience

1. When only one person is wasted and the other has to either deal with the sloppiness or suck it up and wait to get their needs met.

2. When you decide to get it on just because it's a special occasion like a birthday or an anniversary but you'd both secretly rather not, so the sex is less than meh.

3. When someone has cottonmouth and the other's desperate for oral.

4. When your absolute best effort to turn your partner on ends up making them laugh because they're ticklish or just not feeling it.

5. When you realize how awesome hate fucking is, which kind of makes you want to pick more fights.

6. When someone gets caught sneaking a peak at the clock mid sesh.

7. When a weird bodily noise like a queaf makes you both crack up.

8. When an attempt to fake it falls totally flat.

9. When one person wakes up super early feeling incredibly horny so they find a not-so-subtle way to wake up their partner, but they end up pissing them off instead of getting laid.

10. When you get a hot tip about how to make your boyfriend or girlfriend climax like crazy but your execution flops and you feel kind of weird for even trying.

11. When one person isn't at all in the mood but offers their body out of pity anyway.

12. When someone's sick or injured and they decide that sex will make them feel better but they regret initiating intimacy seconds later.

13. When you realize, mid sex, that you're fantasizing about someone other than your significant other—which means that your partner must fantasy cheat on you too sometimes.

14. When someone screams the wrong name by accident and then they have to do their best to convince their partner that they're definitely not *the least bit* attracted to that other man or woman.

15. When someone yawns and then makes the lame claim that it's due to lack of oxygen and not lack of interest.

16. When it hits you that you definitely have a sexual routine as a couple so you freak out that things are getting dull and decide to try a few new positions, but doing so proves super tedious and/or painful.

17. When you happen upon a new badass position inadvertently and pledge to experiment more often.

18. But then you struggle to replicate the experience and get upset that you can't relive the magic.

19. When you misjudge how close your partner is to orgasming so you rush to finish but end up climaxing way too early and get super bored waiting for them to catch up.

20. When one person makes an aggressive future sexual promise just so they can put off intercourse until the next day without getting too much heat about it.

21. When someone breaks out into song or says something in bed indicating that their mind is definitely elsewhere.

22. When one person's totally turned on by a scene in a movie or TV show that the other finds revolting or disturbing.

23. When foreplay forces you to acknowledge that pre-cum is *definitely* a real thing, which makes you rethink the pull-out method all over again.

8

You Have To Evolve Together, Or Go Your Separate Ways

When I think about the person I was eight years ago, back when I first met my boyfriend, I'm shocked that we're still together. It's not that I love my boyfriend any less than I once did, or that our relationship isn't as strong as it once was. It's that I've changed so much in the last eight years, as one does. My interests and needs are completely different from what they once were. Because, in so many ways, *I* was completely different.

Back then, I was mainly searching for release—an outlet from the pain of watching my older sister succumb to alcoholism. I didn't have the emotional capacity for a *real* relationship. I had no bandwidth for commitment or loyalty or the ongoing cycle of quarreling and compromise and resolution that defines romantic love, at least in part. I wanted sex and passion and escape.

So I had an affair.

Truthfully, an illicit sexual relationship was exactly what I needed at that stage in life. I wanted to have sex with a man I was madly attracted to, whose company I thoroughly enjoyed. We had crazy fun times together and that was all and that was enough. There were no loose strings of unaddressed feelings or unmet expectations dangling between us. We were connected by a simple, shared desire to fuck someone we liked *a lot*, but never intended to love. He had a wife, after all, and I didn't get involved with him expecting him to leave her.

But time goes on. Circumstances change. Careers begin and end, friends move, and disease strikes. People like my older sister die, and those of us left in their wake cannot possibly stay the same.

After my sister passed, my romantic needs transformed almost instantaneously. There were holes in my soul that needed filling, maybe. Without my permission, acute feelings sprouted from the empty nooks and crannies of my being. And no matter how steadfastly I ignored the seedlings of their existence, those stubborn little fuckers kept blossoming.

Suddenly, I wanted a *real* relationship, and I wanted it with the married man I'd been sleeping with for several years already. The man I'd once liked but didn't *want* to love quickly became the man I *needed* to love.

When I told him this, he was clearly flattered. But he didn't reciprocate the sentiment, exactly.

Within a year, however, he and his wife had separated.

Falling in love with him was as easy as I knew it would be. I wanted to do whatever he was doing at all times, be with him whenever possible, wherever that took me. I prioritized him above everything else, and I never questioned us.

We continued to have a lot of fun together—maybe even too much. We also started to fight and to compromise and to resolve whatever issues we encountered along our way, as actual couples must. Transitioning from a dalliance to an official relationship was exciting and rewarding. But it also proved tough.

Every relationship transition, I've since realized, is difficult on some level. Moving in together, meeting each other's families, combining finances, marriage, children. No stage, however thrilling, is entirely awesome. Progress never happens without a few growing pains. Why?

Because as circumstances change, people change too. Just as you can't expect your friends, family, career, or interests to remain stagnant, you can't expect your partner to remain fixed as an individual.

As time goes by, you and your partner will both change. You will learn through your experiences, shared and individual. Each of you will mature and develop new ideas and nurture new aspirations.

And at every single turn, you will have to decide whether you can evolve together, or not. You will have to assess whether you can embrace the latest iterations of each other. You will have to determine if your relationship is flexible enough to withstand whatever reshaping is required to move forward as a couple. You will have to do the work it takes to mold a new togetherness over and over and over again, or accept that you're unwilling or incapable of doing that work and go your separate ways.

When considering a long-term partnership with someone, it's insufficient to love who that person is today. You have to ask yourself whether you can love who they'll *become*. Not just whether you can love them in good times and bad, but whether you can love them for who they might be as a result of those hypothetical but inevitable good times and bad.

The thing is, you can't predict who that is.

Life is messy and love is, too. Relationships aren't immutable because people aren't. People promise forever, and then they take it back—not because they're assholes, necessarily, but because they've changed. Or because *you* have.

Ten, twenty, thirty years from now, neither you nor your partner will exist as you are right now. The future you's will not want the exact same things in life as the you's at present do. All you can hope for is that you want to be together enough to figure out how to move on, again and again, without breaking up. That you're stubborn enough to figure your shit out and evolve as a couple. But there are no guarantees in love—not even the til-death-do-us-part kind.

9

25 Tiny Ways The Love Of Your Life Is Bound To Drive You Crazy (Because That's Just Life)

1. They'll spill something on you at a really bad time, like when you're late for work or just not in a *that's-okay-honey-bear!* mindset.

2. They'll do a shit job of cleaning up after they break something and *you'll* pay the price exactly three days later, when you step on a tiny shard of glass that makes you gush vats of blood and proves impossible to excavate.

3. They'll tell you that you said or did something that you definitely didn't say or do. And no matter how much counter evidence you provide, they won't budge from their rickety, *that's-what-happened-sweetie!* pedestal.

4. They will stubbornly refuse to believe you about something related to a topic that falls within *your* area of expertise.

5. They'll remember a joint experience incorrectly but insist that they're right so emphatically that you'll question your sanity a little.

6. They'll fail to remember a moment from your history as a couple that you've long considered important. As you pile on the descriptive details in a desperate attempt to trigger an *aha!* in your best friend slash lover, they'll look back at you with a blank face, rendering that oh-so-special moment totally meaningless.

7. They'll wake up in an amazing mood on a day you're feeling *meh* for whatever reason, which will make wallowing in your sad face state of mind that much ickier.

8. They'll ask you to fetch something that's obviously closer to wherever they're situated at the time.

9. They'll insist on showing you how yellow or green their snot is when you're not at all in the mood to stomach gross stuff.

10. They will fail to laugh at a joke you find hilarious, thereby robbing you of anticipated glory.

11. They'll take a super long, steamy shower when you're desperate to get on with your own grooming routine.

12. They'll finish the milk right before you can pour a smidge into your morning coffee.

13. They'll buy the wrong brand of toilet paper or tampons or body lotion or some other product you're VERY particular about for good reason.

14. They'll reveal something to your friends or family that you've told them a million times over to keep secret.

15. They'll hate an outfit you genuinely love. You won't change clothes, but you will feel less joy wearing them.

16. They'll ask you to throw something out that you treasure, like a piece of artwork you purchased before getting together or a teddy bear you're not quite ready to part with.

17. They'll spend money on something you definitely don't want or need and the item will only be returnable for store credit.

18. They'll suggest going to a movie that ends up sucking.

19. They'll think you're angry when you're definitely not and then try to make you happy but their well-intentioned overtures will be super annoying and, ironically, angering.

20. They'll embarrass you, by accident or not, at a time when you're not at all in the mood to be humiliated.

21. They'll take credit for something you're definitely responsible for.

22. They'll fail to read your save-me-from-crazy signals at a party, leaving you to suffer in the company of someone dreadful.

23. They'll think they've won an argument they definitely didn't win and their false sense of satisfaction will irk you more than whatever caused you to fight in the first place.

24. Their selective hearing will kick in at the least opportune time, like when you shout a critical request as you rush out the door. Or they'll mishear you at a time when every single syllable of instructions is absolutely critical.

25. Worse yet, they'll hear you but totally misconstrue the meaning behind your words and they'll be confused, hurt, or mad as hell as a result. Then you'll have to explain yourself a bazillion times over until they finally get it. Or at least stop caring.

10

21 Brutal Relationship Truths Healthy Couples Accept (Because They Know They Have To)

1. The best gift you can give your partner is to wake up every day and be the best version of your authentic self. But there will be days when you're inexplicably grumpy and there's absolutely nothing the love of your life can do to make it better except sit there and tolerate you.

2. Loving someone means caring enough to give them the space they need to be an asshole or a curmudgeon some days for no apparent reason—to appreciate them when they're at their darkest as well as their happiest. You won't like your boyfriend or girlfriend all the time, but you won't like yourself every day, either.

3. No matter how compatible you are, you won't agree on everything simply because you're two different people. You'll disagree on political candidates, throw pillows, and how much salt to use while cooking.

4. And because you're both destined to change over time, the person you're dating might start to look different from the person you fell for to start with, which can be scary. Since we evolve as a function of our experiences (some shared, some not), the person you love today might very well develop new interests, hobbies, habits, or opinions that you don't very much like.

5. That means that you will absolutely have to compromise regularly. You will have to bargain on an ongoing basis, accepting the rug you only sort of like in exchange for the right to keep the teddy bear your boyfriend or girlfriend despises displayed on the bed year round.

6. Sometimes, you won't even be able to reach a compromise. You will negotiate yourselves into a corner, at which point you might have to rely on measures like rock-paper-scissors or a good ol' coin toss.

7. And you will have to accept defeat sometimes, because you will *not* win every round of rock-paper-scissors or every coin toss because that's life.

8. Your partner is definitely going to offend you occasionally—sometimes on purpose, during a massive fight because they just can't help themselves, and sometimes totally by accident.

9. There's no one better positioned to hit you with the lowest of low blows than the person you love the most in life because they know you better than anyone else. If you abuse

your power to cut deep, you have to expect an equally cruel response.

10. Sometimes, your partner will say or do something foolish in public. It's your job to cover for them as best you can, and to love the fuck out of them regardless.

11. Because sometimes, you're going to make a fool of yourself, and you'll need their support whenever that happens.

12. There's a time and a place for honesty. Sometimes, when your partner tells a joke that falls totally flat, they'll need you to fake laugh in response to make them feel good. And if they ask whether they look okay as they rush out the door, there's only one right answer.

13. You will both probably covet other people sexually, and that's okay. You're both human, so you're both susceptible to crushing on other people and/or lusting after their bodies.

14. Flirting can be innocent, and entertaining naughty thoughts about strangers, colleagues, or even friends doesn't mean you love your significant other any less.

15. Because love doesn't make you immune to temptation. Resisting temptation takes work on an ongoing basis, and there's no shame in that.

16. It's up to you and your partner to set boundaries you're both comfortable with, and to honor those boundaries to the best of your abilities.

17. No matter what, you will both fuck up. You will hurt each other over and over again because people make mistakes no matter how old they get, or how good they are at heart.

18. There will be painful times riddled with doubts and apologies and breakdowns. Times when you will have to wonder whether or not your partner will be able to forgive you, or decide to move on instead. There are never any guarantees that a person will stay with you forever, even if you're married.

19. And you can never be 100 percent certain about what's going on in your significant other's head. Even if you feel a connection to your partner that's stronger than anything you've ever known, their mind will always be their own.

20. Similarly, your relationship will always be unique from every other couple's, and there will only be two people who ever truly get it: you, and them.

21. Although it's natural to make comparisons, no one is perfect and no relationship is ideal, no matter what anyone's carefully curated social media feed says.

11

50 'What Ifs' Even The Most Compatible Couples Need To Consider Before Settling Down Together Forever

1. What if one of us desperately craves some kind of change, but the other's completely content with the status quo?

2. What if we develop separate hobbies or interests that aren't at all conducive to spending time together?

3. What'll we do if we end up making enough money to stop working way before we thought possible?

4. What if we get *really* rich? Like, hit-the-jackpot multi-millionaire wealthy?

5. What if only one of us achieves professional success in their chosen field?

6. What if one person continues to struggle while the other finds contentment in life overall?

7. What if we decide to launch a business together and it takes off, but also compromises our relationship along the way?

8. What if we realize that we're even better business partners than lovers?

9. What if one of us develops the urge to do something sexually that makes the other person uncomfortable?

10. What if we want entirely different things in bed at a certain stage?

11. What if one person has a breakthrough that leads them to question everything they once believed?

12. What if someone's secret is revealed and the information uncovered is disappointing or unsettling or unforgivable?

13. What if we evolve into totally different people from who we are today?

14. What if one person desperately wants a dog, but the other's intent on a cat, or a goldfish?

15. What if one of us decides to embrace a super restrictive diet that makes eating out totally un-fun?

16. What if we develop the itch to travel somewhere but we can't really afford to take the trip?

17. What if we decide to have kids, but can't get pregnant?

18. What if we have to downsize and live way more humbly than we ever anticipated?

19. What if we lose *everything*?

20. What if one of us gets laid off or fired?

21. What if one of us decides to shift professional gears late in life?

22. What if either of us wants to go back to school suddenly?

23. What if one of us experiences an unanticipated religious awakening?

24. What if one of us befriends someone the other strongly dislikes?

25. What if one of us develops a questionably close friendship with someone of the opposite sex?

26. What if one of us feels unloved or disrespected by the other's family?

27. What if one of us gets into a massive fight with someone we both adore?

28. What if we strongly disagree about how to handle an important family matter?

29. What if one of starts to hate where we live but the other is adamantly against relocating?

30. What if our house burns down, literally?

31. What if we find ourselves at the center of some Hurricane Katrina grade natural disaster?

32. What if we disagree vehemently about who should be President during a heated election?

33. What if one of us ages way faster than the other and we start to look like we're a decade apart even if we're not?

34. What if either of us develops an addiction?

35. What if one person becomes seriously ill unexpectedly?

36. What if one of us gets into a horrible freak accident and ends up alive, but comatose?

37. What if one of us loses a limb?

38. What if one person dies way before their time, leaving the other behind?

39. What if we lose a close friend or relative unexpectedly?

40. What if one of us is the victim of a terrible crime?

41. What if one of us is accused of a crime (falsely or not)?

42. What if we witness a horrible act and have to enter the Witness Protection Program to save our family?

43. What if something goes horribly wrong during a routine procedure either of us is undergoing?

44. What if one of us is being sexually harassed at work?

45. What if one of us has to work crazy long hours for an extended period, or travel extensively for professional reasons?

46. What if one of us starts to feel unloved, lonely, or neglected?

47. What if one of us just can't shake the blues?

48. What if we start to forget why we got together in the first place?

49. What if we completely disagree on whose side to take when our friends split up or divorce?

50. What if we get closer and closer as the years go by and stop fighting altogether and our relationship happiness makes everyone around us want to projectile vomit?

12

Cute Or Creepy? 17 Adorably Weird Things Healthy Couples Secretly Do Together

1. They burst into song regularly, even if they have terrible voices, because they're not at all insecure in each other's company and sometimes life calls for bursting into song randomly.

2. They dance for each other naked sometimes—to be silly, not sexy. Because few things are funnier than watching your partner do an impromptu nude jig, and each person in the relationship is fully committed to self-mockery in the name of joint laughter.

3. They wrestle, vigorously but affectionately, because loving each other so deeply results in excess energy that needs an outlet. When they end up entangled in a strange pretzel like formation on the couch or the bed, they remain there for a few minutes longer than necessary, happy to be (literally) knotted in love.

4. They leave each other love notes in odd places—in shoes and pockets, on the back wall of the medicine cabinet, or scribbled in red lipstick across the bathroom mirror. These tiny thoughtful gestures, though redundant, never lose their power to surprise or delight.

5. They do things as a team that could easily be done solo—like chop vegetables, take out the trash, or check the mail—because doing so makes them feel closer and more connected, even for just a few moments.

6. They invent bedtime stories starring each other. These tales might be recreations of memorable past events, or hypotheticals surrounding their shared future. Whatever the case, there's something supremely comforting about them.

7. They tend to make up words to express how passionately they feel about each other because the dictionary's existing options all seem so insufficient.

8. They're given to making up weird games, too. Understanding the importance of play, they're eager to turn life's duller moments into fun. But if they race or compete, it's for the thrill of it, never out of anger or a desire to outdo each other.

9. If one person falls asleep prematurely, the other stares longingly at their peaceful drooling partner, considering how lucky they are—believing, in fact, that they're the most fortunate man or woman alive. They honestly prefer each other in this natural, no fuss state.

10. They share things that aren't designed to be shared, like toothbrushes, washcloths, and razors. The act of sharing when it's unnecessary seems especially intimate.

11. They prefer to pack their belongings together rather than take separate suitcases because they like the idea of their stuff touching just as much as they like the idea of touching each other constantly.

12. They tag each other in ridiculous posts on social media and make inside jokes in the comments that strike everyone else as cryptic or cheesy. Luckily, they honestly don't care what anyone else thinks.

13. They dream about each other frequently—sometimes sexually and sometimes not—because their lives are so intricately intertwined. The only thing better than dreaming about each other is waking up to recount the bizarre details of their subconscious minds.

14. They prank each other whenever possible, addicted to the high and the challenge of cracking each other up. The relationship is partly an ongoing exercise in executing increasingly complicated, well-intentioned practical jokes.

15. They doctor photos and construct meme like graphics that will never be shared outside the relationship because they're purely designed for viewing as a couple.

16. They monitor each other's appearance on a granular level, casually pointing out pimples and stray hairs or odd little bumps as they arise. They'll even excavate ingrown hairs or shave each other in certain areas upon request.

17. Sometimes, when they're out in public where no one knows them—at a restaurant, a sporting event, or the bank—they pretend to be husband and wife. They play married couple for kicks, and because they're eager on some level to reach that stage in life (if they haven't already, that is).

13

10 Things That Stress You Out In A New Relationship (That You Get To Stop Caring About Six Months Later)

1. The awareness that you're being vetted every second you're together.

Before you become an official couple, you have to endure the process of vetting (and being vetted by) the person you're dating. Being the best version of your authentic self every time you meet up with someone requires time, energy, and a whole lot of willpower. It's fucking exhausting, but hopefully the adrenaline rush of starting something promising pushes you through. The good news? If you make it past the six-month mark, the pressure not to burp and fart in front of each other tends to evaporate.

2. Going "number two" and stinking up their bathroom.

No one wants to be associated with fouls smells early in a relationship. You want your new partner to think of you as a bouquet of flowers perfuming their life with a lovely, intoxicating scent. So if holding your bowel movement for an extra half hour affords you the opportunity to go number two at a café or a bar or restaurant or even a friend's place instead of theirs, you'll deal with the temporary discomfort. People go to great lengths to avoid producing icky smells during the wooing phase—until romance transitions into reality, and you both realize that the children's storybook *Everyone Poops* is totally accurate.

3. What your web presence says about you.

Since incessant documenting is the norm these days, each of us leaves a long, telling trail of content for others (especially potential significant others), to comb through online. Even if you stand by every single Tweet and social media post, thinking about your web presence through someone else's eyes will probably freak you out. You'll want to explain certain things—like why you look totally out of it in the middle of the day in that one photo, or why you Tweeted directly at Taylor Swift that one time last Summer—to give the guy or girl you're dating some context. Or you might just engage in some frenzied deleting and caption editing to curate a more acceptable version of the online you. About six months down the line, you'll remember that everyone should withhold judgment unless they want to be peered at through the same overcritical lens.

4. Knowing that they dated other people before you.

Before you reach the secure phase as a couple, you will fixate on the people your new partner dated before they were lucky enough to meet you. Until you know someone fully, it makes sense to define them at least in part by the romantic ~~mistakes~~ choices they've made. What does that mean? You will probably ask your new boo direct questions about all their exes under the guise of curiosity and/or a quasi sincere desire to know *everything* about them. Unfortunately, everything you learn about all those other people they dated will make you highly uncomfortable.

5. What you discover from cyberstalking their exes.

You will probably cyberstalk each and every one of your partner's exes—an activity that is neither fun nor interesting, let alone confidence boosting. You'll do it regardless because you just can't help yourself, racking up a slew of unfounded concerns along the way. The second you stop stressing about your predecessors, you'll know you've reached a new stage of relationship seriousness.

6. How to phrase each and every text message.

There's a very fine line between expressing enthusiasm about a budding relationship and coming across as overly needy and/or borderline insane. So the simple act of communicating—replying to a text or returning a phone call or commenting on someone's social media post—takes on new meaning in the early stages of dating. You will read and re-read each other's messages, trying to extrapolate more hidden truth than so few characters can possibly hold. You might even phone a friend to ask for phrasing advice before realizing that you're perfectly capable of drafting a reply to "What are you up to this weekend?" all by your grownup self.

7. How much physical affection you can show—without seeming clingy.

No one wants to be the crazy one who gets too attached too soon. But no one wants to be the indifferent one incapable of demonstrating a modicum of affection, either. So you'll hesitate over every little intimate gesture in the beginning—from holding hands on the way to dinner to upper thigh rubbing during a movie and making out in public. The sooner you figure out just how much physical touch your boyfriend or girlfriend needs to feel loved without feeling smothered, and just how PDA friendly they are, the better.

8. How to get their friends to like you.

If you want the boyfriend or girlfriend slot in someone's life, you don't just have to win them over. You have to convince their friends, too. So the first few nights spent double dating or hanging out with someone's nearest and dearest will be some of the most stressful. It's one thing to be your best self in a one-on-one scenario, and another to play "definitely worth dating" before a small crowd of your would-be significant other's biggest fans. Convincing someone's squad that you're datable is flat-out exhausting, but you've got to do it if you want a decent chance at phase two.

9. What you wear every single time you see them.

Outfit choices matter a lot in the beginning. You want to look put together, clean-cut, and attractive. And you don't want to wear the same thing twice in a row, or within too short a timespan. At the same time, you don't want to be seen as someone who cares too much about clothing. So you expend a tremendous amount of effort getting ready before every date, and even more effort feigning wardrobe indifference while taking mental notes about your sartorial choices to avoid future repeats. Hopefully it's not too long before you're back to t-shirts and jeans, and turning your underwear inside out to make it last one more day.

10. How to come across as the most well mannered version of yourself.

When dining with someone you're still getting to know, it's beneficial to be perceived as polite. Typically, that means being way more mindful of the manners your parents ingrained in you than usual. Napkin on the lap shortly after being seated? Check. Elbows on the table? No way. And even though you desperately want to order the steak (but only if you can swap the home fries for the regular kind), you go with the salmon because you'd rather have your second choice than seem overly fussy for requesting a menu substitution. Luckily, by the six month mark you'll be freed from pretending to be anything other than your picky, finger licking self.

14

10 Tips On How To Live With Someone For The Rest Of Your Life Without Going Fucking Crazy

1. Be up front about your pet peeves, and agree not to push each other's buttons.

Maybe you can't stand nail biting, or you hate overhearing phone conversations with customer service agents, or the sight of an unfolded towel or an uncapped Listerine bottle drives you Britney-Spears-circa-2007 insane. It doesn't matter how weird or irrational your pet peeves are. When you're sharing a home with another imperfect human, you have to be honest about all the tiny little things that make you want to stab your own eyes out with a toothpick. Then you have to ask your partner to avoid doing those things in exchange for the reassurance that you will try your best to avoid doing whatever makes *them* want to dive into an empty pool. Otherwise, you might just kill each other.

2. Pledge to have sex regularly—even when you can't stand each other.

If you're sharing a bed with someone, there's no reason not to have sex several times a week. Sexual intimacy triggers the brain's feel good hormones, urging you to associate pleasant sensations with the person you're banging. Bottom line: You're ten thousand percent less likely to annoy the fuck out of each other if you're fucking consistently. You don't even have to be on good terms to reap the benefits of bumping uglies. And if the value of maintaining a peaceful relationship isn't enough to sell you on the idea of routine lovemaking, consider nooky a favor to yourself. Because even if you're pissed at the person who gives it to you, an orgasm is pretty much always awesome.

3. Don't be afraid to go to bed angry.

All healthy couples fight, and when resolution doesn't come quickly, things can devolve into nasty don't-expect-your-desert-vagina-to-get-wet-anytime-soon-because-I-can't-stand-you territory that's typically better left unexplored. If you sense that you're not going to see things your partner's way as bedtime approaches, go the fuck to sleep. Because the only thing worse than two angry people butting heads is two exhausted, angry people failing to play nice. When you choose sleep over prolonging a battle, chances are the urge to strangle each other will subside overnight so you can start fresh the next day.

4. Apologize after every single fight.

If you want to live well with another human being whose loveable quirks are sometimes just as difficult to stomach as your own, you absolutely have to take responsibility for your role in every skirmish, large and small. When two people fight, both parties are always culpable on some level and if you don't own your part of the ugliness, you can't expect the other person to. You don't need to rehash the particulars of a quarrel to say a simple "sorry," which can go a long way in propelling a couple forward. Otherwise, issues quickly accumulate into stacks of unresolved emotional grudges that will definitely topple one day.

5. Clean up after yourselves.

Hopefully you're at least somewhat aligned with your significant other on the pig-to-neat-freak spectrum. No matter where you each fall, it's important to do your best to clean up your own messes. No one wants to live with someone who can't prepare a snack for themselves without leaving a sticky disaster behind on the kitchen counter. So whether or not you're anal about keeping the lids of peanut butter jars goo free, be mindful that you're home isn't just your own. You're equally responsible for keeping it as neat and cockroach free as possible.

6. Make sure each person has a space that's entirely their own.

You don't have to live in a mansion to carve out a separate nook for each person to decorate as an expression of their identity. Having your own space lets you maintain some semblance of individuality once you exchange your first person singular existence for the this-is-what-*we're*-up-to life of a cohabiting couple. Respect each other's right to retreat to this personal space whenever necessary.

7. Don't let dated gender norms dictate the division of labor.

When deciding who should tackle which household chores, don't fall into the trap of making sex-based assumptions. It might just be that doing the dishes after dinner relaxes a man, while taking a short walk to empty the trash appeals to a woman, and mowing the lawn is something you'll have to outsource since neither of you are willing to inhale bits of grass. Be honest about which tasks are the least off-putting to you and volunteer your services to vacuum or clean the toilet without worrying which chores are traditionally male or female. Buckets, mops, and brooms don't have genitals anyway.

8. Don't expect a medal for every chore you cross of your joint To Do list.

We all thrive off of flattery, but fishing for compliments or affirmation is tedious. If you need a pat on the back for every errand you run or unpleasant job you complete, consider giving it to yourself or call home to mom. You're on the same tea, but your partner isn't your personal cheerleader, so don't expect them to praise you for every little thing you accomplish. Unless things are divided unequally, your significant other is doing just as much as you are to make your shared home a liveable place.

9. Play to your individual strengths in managing the nitty-gritty.

Existing in the modern world requires dealing with a lot of minutiae—from banking to grocery shopping and choosing the right cell phone carrier. When you're single, you have to handle *everything* yourself. The advantage of managing day-to-day life as a duo is that you can split regular duties according to which annoying details you hate dealing with the least. By assigning loose roles like Minister of Technology, Head of Finance, Entertainment Chair, and Director of Culture according to each person's knowledge base and skill set, you can spare each other from fretting over some of the more irksome aspects of adulthood, like signing up for the most sensible mobile phone plan, and remembering to buy tickets to that concert the second they go on sale.

10. Proactively adopt each other's good habits.

Some people are very mindful of their diet while others are good about exercising, calling their parents weekly, or keeping a tidy house. If you've chosen to cohabit, hopefully you admire at least a few things about your partner's approach to life. But don't count on your significant other's best habits seeping through your skin by way of breathing the same air. Identify what your boyfriend or girlfriend does better than you and commit to trying those things their way. If you embrace your partner's commendable habits and note their life enhancing impact on your life, you'll have an easier time coping with the less awesome aspects of living with someone for the rest of your life.

15

19 Signs Your Relationship Is (Pretty Much) Stronger Than The Green Monster

1. You don't (usually) bother cyberstalking your significant other because you have so many better things to do than agonize over (mostly) nothing.

2. You don't (usually) bother cyberstalking their exes, either, because you honestly don't care if your partner's in touch with a few past flames (as long as they're keeping everything absolutely PG).

3. You dream about each other constantly, but when one of you admits to fantasizing about someone else, the other person finds it more hilarious than threatening (as soon as they get past the initial shock). It's just a dream, after all, and you both know that brains do super weird things.

4. You can tell each other (almost) anything without fearing judgment, so you share (a large percentage of) your darkest thoughts, confess (many of) your biggest mistakes, and (sometimes) mention offhandedly that you masturbated earlier in the day.

5. When logistics prevent you from having sex for longer than you'd like, neither of you entertains the urge to stray (for all that long) or obsesses (all that much) over the thought that the other might resort to cheating.

6. The truth is that you'd both rather wait for each other than be intimate with anyone else, so you can totally handle bouts of sexual frustration (as long as they're definitely temporary).

7. Once you remember that there's value in pleasure delay, you actually (kind of) appreciate the opportunity to ache for your partner's naked body.

8. You tend to get FOMO when you can't go out with your significant other, but you don't get (all that) jealous or suspicious, knowing in your heart that there's (almost) nothing to worry about.

9. Even if one person looks especially hot on their way to dinner or the office, there's (not necessarily) direct questioning about the intention behind a sexy outfit.

10. If anything, you (sort of) like that your partner draws attention from the opposite sex, even when you're not around.

11. You're not dumb to the fact that temptations exist, but you don't (typically) fixate on upsetting hypotheticals.

12. Instead, you trust in each other, and in your uniquely close bond (unless of course there's a solid reason not to).

13. You recognize how awesomely marketable your partner is, but you also know that they're one thousand percent committed to your coupledom (on most occasions).

14. Of course there are other awesome people out there, but what exists between you two is (nearly) impossible to replicate, and you both sincerely want what you already have.

15. Occasionally, you point out other hot men and women to each other and neither of you gets (all that) offended, and then you dissect them together like specimens for fun because you're strong enough (for the most part) to accept that you're both physically attracted to other people.

16. When someone compliments your significant other's appearance or personality, you don't (typically) fret over the would-be seductress or suitor. Instead, you feel (mostly) flattered, viewing your significant other as an extension of yourself.

17. You fight passionately, but always (wherein "always" is loosely defined) with the end in sight. Though it seems far off sometimes, peace is (usually) on the horizon, somewhere behind all the stink eyes and biting comebacks.

18. When friends gush about how amazing their current relationship is, you listen intently but secretly doubt that whatever they have measures up to what you've got (when things are going great).

19. You consider yourself part of the couple others emulate, and you sincerely wish that everyone you love finds something as special as you guys have (on good days).

16

9 Ways Men Push The Boundaries Of Fidelity Without Technically Cheating (The Way They See It)

1. They have emotional "affairs."

Whether he's messaging a former flame to wax nostalgic about the past, or getting to know a 20-something Kansan bombshell who happens to share his interest in anime, things can get intimate quickly when you interact with someone often enough on an emotional level. A lot of men write off their non-physical relationships as benign, no matter how close they get, simply because the in-person component is missing. The questionable aspect of nurturing an emotional connection, either over the Internet or in real life, is that doing so requires time and energy that could conceivably be spent with a man's actual partner. Plus, it's tough to ignore the possibility that things might get *too* personal, even from a distance. It's not like love hasn't sprouted all across the Internet already.

2. They plan dinners with female friends that could easily be lunch dates.

When scheduling plans to meet up with a female friend, a man faces a simple choice: Request getting together for coffee or lunch, or suggest drinks and/or dinner. Sometimes, a man chooses the latter when the former is just as feasible. Why? Because afternoon meet-ups are safe and boring, and few people are willing to get stupid and tipsy midday. It's fun to booze and flirt with a female pal sometimes, and it seems harmless enough, even it means skipping dinner with the ball and chain.

3. They buy drinks for strangers.

At some point most men will end up having a cocktail or a beer at a bar by themselves, either because they're traveling for work, or they decide to stop off for a moment of peace on their way home. If an attractive woman happens to be sitting a few seats down, sending her a drink might seem like the generous, gentlemanly thing to do—a simple way to earn a smile from a hot stranger. Next? An invitation to join him for a second drink or a nightcap down the street so he can engage her in conversation, stare at her cleavage, and dust off his inner lothario for a bit. Things might end right there, and they may not.

4. They maintain relationships with office wives.

It's nice to have someone to gossip with about colleagues, to vent to about your boss, and to confide in day to day. Since only those who understand your working environment can appreciate certain aspects of your daily life, it makes sense for anyone to develop a close personal relationship with one of their fellow employees. When such a bond is formed with a member of the opposite sex, however, the inter-office relationship can start to seem remarkably spousal. As innocent as a man's intentions may be to start, he probably spends a large percentage of time with his female coworker slash wife. Keeping things purely platonic with an office spouse isn't always simple.

5. They share their favorite porn with other women.

Pornography is ubiquitous, and we know that tons of men and women watch it at least once in a while. That said, most of us aren't in the habit of discussing our exact porn watching habits in everyday conversation. The man who shares his favorite X-rated video(s) with a woman who isn't his significant other probably justifies doing so as flirting at arm's length—as a way to be sensual with someone he's attracted to without ever touching her (but maybe touching himself while he envisions her masturbating to his fave smut). When a man reveals what material he uses to get aroused, he divulges part of his personal erotic profile. A relatively innocuous act, perhaps. But how long can a porn swap between adults go on before things escalate?

6. They reveal their sexual dreams and/or fantasies to female friends.

We all entertain dirty thoughts about our celebrity crushes, hot colleagues, old partners, and even our dads since our brains aren't equipped to screen for incest while we sleep. There's no such thing as a "bad" thought, right? Just bad actions. So why shouldn't I share my dirty thoughts with the woman who played the lead in my hard-core dream, a man might wonder. Why not flatter a woman if she's the type to respond well to a little naughty talk? Many would argue that there's a significant difference between entertaining dirty fantasies and detailing the particulars to another party, but not the man on a mission to push a boundary.

7. They hire virtual girlfriends.

Does having sex with an artificially intelligent robot qualify as cheating? It's tough to say, but we're not quite there yet as a society, technologically speaking. Still, there are plenty of ways men can use tech to get sexy. A few options include paying for the "girlfriend experience" through a service like GirlfriendHire, dropping tokens on My Free Cams, and dicking around on Craiglist. These days, a digital fling isn't out of anyone's price range.

8. They go all out at strip clubs.

Women tend to think of hitting up a strip club as a single sport, but there are so many variations in how a man might approach a visit to a nudie bar. He might wander in casually for a steak dinner and a few drinks so he can play spectator for an hour and skip the lap dances altogether. He might head over late night with a bunch of buddies and let them go wild as he sits, sipping his vodka tonic, happy to get drunk and watch others squander their money. Or he might go on a bender himself, spending an entire paycheck to motor-boat a lady's breasts over and over. Some men come in their pants while naked women grind on them at a strip joint. Others don't. Whatever their preferred strip club style, however, men tend to agree that strip clubs are an acceptable form of entertainment, whether or not they have girlfriends, who may or may not share the same philosophy.

9. They get "happy endings."

The truth is, it's not all that (ahem) hard for the average man to justify paying for a happy ending. A rub-and-tug can seem like the natural extension of an intensely relaxing massage specifically designed to *release* tension. It's not like there's any emotion involved in booking a basic spa appointment. Plus, spas are about health and wellness! It's easy to see why a man who pays his masseuse to jack him off would feel mostly renewed rather than guilty. Or is it?

17

23 Unromantic Realities You Have To Accept If You Want Lasting Love

1. You won't always feel loving towards your significant other. There will be moments when you say you do, but it's not exactly, entirely true.

2. You won't always be sexually attracted to them, either.

3. In fact, sometimes you'll look at your partner and feel nothing but sincere disgust and rage, bordering on hate.

4. Indifference, not hate, is the opposite of love, you'll have to remind yourself. A comforting thought when things get dark—and believe me, they will.

5. The quirks you've always adored in your partner might very well annoy the fuck out of you once in a while.

6. Even a person's most beautiful features and loveliest traits can seem unimaginably irritating if they're behaving in a way that drives you crazy, or if you're stuck in the rut of a terrible mood for whatever reason.

7. The truth is, no one has bottomless reserves of love and adoration—not you or your partner, no matter how smitten you are with each other. Not anyone.

8. You'll both probably text a few old flames routinely, usually in the aftermath of a fight, to make yourselves feel better about life. And you may or may not feel guilty about doing so.

9. As a species we crave novelty, and it's impossible to get it from a single person on an ongoing basis.

10. When things aren't going so well, you'll probably daydream about leaving your significant other to be with someone else. Relationship problems tend to make old boyfriends and office crushes seem like really great prospects.

11. You *will* doubt your relationship. You will question whether your long-term boyfriend or girlfriend, husband or wife really understands you. Appreciates you. Deserves you.

12. Loving someone doesn't mean accepting every aspect of that person's character. So you might never grow to love *everything* about your significant other, even if you say you do.

13. Your partner probably won't be enough to make you feel whole, or completely happy. That's what friends are for—to fill the gaps left by romantic relationships.

14. Your significant other is bound to lie to you on more than one occasion—about where they are, what they're doing, or how much money they've spent. Because people lie, especially when doing so is the path of least resistance.

15. They're also going to entertain a lot of unsavory thoughts about people who aren't you. Because they're human.

16. Marital vows are moving, but they're not unbreakable.

17. All those wedding toasts *do* mean something, but they *don't* mean that any couple is better positioned than the others that have fielded remarkably similar comments, all from friends and family, regarding the strength of their bonds.

18. Wedding celebrations are fun, but they're an exercise in collective denial—that the man and woman recently hitched will be able to do things differently, to avoid the marital struggles every couple eventually encounters.

19. If you're certain that you'll avoid the relationship traps others fall into—that you'll manage to do better than everyone else—you're delusional.

20. Love is the source of so much beauty, but it also causes insufferable pain.

21. Some days, you'll have to try really hard to love your partner. And that's okay.

22. Love is a great reason to maintain a relationship, but on its own, it's insufficient. Staying together requires *a lot* of hard work.

23. You have to choose to put the effort in to be with someone long-term again and again—to love them even when you don't.

18

10 Weird Things That Happen During Sex When You're Monogamous For Long Enough

1. Someone will fart.

There's a direct correlation between how close you grow as a couple, and how much less effort each party devotes to holding their farts in. This mathematical reality holds true inside and outside the bedroom. Farting freely can be wonderfully intimate! But it can also be awkward, especially in the middle of a passionate romp. Letting one rip during sex simply isn't something you can avoid forever. For the sake of preserving the mood, you might try to keep a mid-sex toot silent, but even so, you're bound to stink things up a little.

2. Someone will drizzle nose juice all over the other.

Mucus dripping is another bodily function we can't control at all times. Whether it's allergy season and you're prone to sudden sneezing, or you're just recovering from a cold and you want that orgasm you've been missing while lying sick in bed so damn badly so you have sex while sniffly, you're at high risk of uncontrollable nose goo dribbling. And unless it's your own, snot is pretty gross. So don't expect your significant other to mask their disgust after you drizzle all over them. The best thing to do is keep a box of tissues next to the bed so you can promptly wipe up your nasal juices from wherever they happen to land on your partner's body.

3. An attempt at naughty talk will fall totally flat.

The problem with becoming well versed in the art of dirty talk is that doing so requires practice and a certain willingness to experiment, which invariably leads to small failures. What sounds sexy to one person might sound ridiculous to another. And you can't distinguish the relative effectiveness of "My pussy is hugging your cock" versus "I'm squeezing my vagina muscles *so* tight for you, baby" until you market test both. No matter how much you love your boyfriend or girlfriend, it can be super awkward to see their brow furrow in response to a carefully crafted phrase intended to arouse rather than confuse. (A tip from personal experience: slang words like "cock" and "dick" are generally preferable to medical textbook terms like "penis" and "testicles.")

4. There will be an accidental knock on the "backdoor."

You've gone through the motions of foreplay and you're both hot and ready for penis insertion. Since a woman's vagina and anus are mere inches apart, it would be unreasonable to expect total accuracy every single time a guy tries to stick it inside. Every man is likely to misfire on occasion and poke his girlfriend in the backdoor. Depending on how a woman feels about anal play, such misguided hole navigation may be received as an unexpected but welcome foray into butt sex territory, or a traumatic, unforgivable mistake.

5. You will mishandle each other's private parts.

As much time as you spend hooking up, you're never going to be as familiar with the opposite sex's private parts as you are with your own anatomy, which you get to poke and prod on the sly constantly. As a result, there will be times when you're trying to arouse your partner by fondling their genitals but you're so far off base, it's bound to become embarrassing. Your sensual massage might just tickle them, and that sudden rub, yank, or grab might produce an "ow!" instead of the intended satisfied moan.

6. Someone will scream the wrong name.

You love each other to bits, but you both spend *a lot* of time around other people, and they all have names. Your friends, colleagues, and family members all compete for your attention daily. So many different monikers pop up in your inbox and social media feeds every single minute! You can't always be expected to think and say the right one while you're in bed with your lover. But as easy as it is to understand *why* a case of mistaken identity might happen in the sack, it will always kind of suck.

7. A new sexual position will feel absolutely awesome—to exactly *one* of you.

One of the joys of being in a long-term relationship is trying new positions out in the name of staving off the sexual boredom that often accompanies monogamy. When you have sex with the same person for long enough, you even end up contorting into odd positions you've never seen diagrammed, which you should feel free to name yourselves (personal favorite: The Ice Cream Sandwich). Varying positions is a wonderful way to keep things fresh, except when you get tangled into a human pretzel situation that feels AMAZING to one of you, but hurts like hell for the other. When your bodies don't seem to agree, it can be disheartening, not to mention super painful.

8. One person will fail to get and/or stay in the mood.

You've got a million things going on at all times, so it's natural for certain unsexy thoughts to invade your mind while you're going at it. Sometimes, it will seem nearly impossible to shelve all other concerns for the twenty or so minutes it takes to get naked and boink. Did you remember to cancel that Saturday night dinner reservation? Did you order those light bulbs, or are they still sitting in your Amazon cart? Is tomorrow your bestie's birthday, or is it the next day? Most of the time, you'll manage to keep these unwelcome thoughts to yourself and tuck them aside in time to climax. But occasionally, you're bound to slip up and say something like "Did you ever call your mom back?" out loud at the least awesome moment, effectively advertising to your partner that your head is in more of a future-mother-in-law place than a fuck-me-please state. Whether or not you can bounce back from such a scenario depends on your ability to shift gears as a couple—fast.

9. Someone will nod off unexpectedly and/or yawn.

Many modern men and women work very hard, and they don't get enough sleep as a result. By the time we climb into bed at night, we're often so exhausted that we can't imagine committing an ounce of energy to physical activity, even if the reward is an orgasm. Having sex with your partner when you're supremely tired because you can sense how horny they are is a lovely, selfless thing to do. But there's a risk to opening up shop when you're feeling extremely sleepy. Especially if you're lying flat on your back, you might just nod off while your partner does the humping. The only thing worse than letting your eyelids close momentarily—which, if executed carefully, can be written off as a response to the mind-blowing pleasure you're currently experiencing—is giving into a giant yawn. The "I just need oxygen" line won't get you very far in convincing your partner that you're not totally bored.

10. One of you will experience an ill-timed laughing fit.

Intimacy is often forged through shared hilarious experiences and cracking up with your boyfriend or girlfriend during sex can make for some precious memories. However, if the chuckles are one-sided, they tend to be irritating rather than pleasant. And guess what? You're not always going to find the same things humorous. When you're the only one experiencing a laughing fit—because your partner does something inadvertently funny while trying to arouse you through nipple pinching, maybe—your partner will feel excluded as you take your solo trip down the giggly path. No one likes to feel left out, so unilateral laughing is likely to end in a begrudging, "let's try this again later" disaster.

19

21 Unpleasant Truths Healthy Couples Are Better Off Never Thinking About

1. Your partner's sexual prowess partly stems from experiences they've had with other people. Because unless you're both extremely pure, or you're dating your high school sweetheart, you've both had sex with several other people.

2. That means your naked bodies have rubbed against others', your mouths have engulfed others' private parts, and you've whispered intimate sweet nothings into other people's ears.

3. Some of your previous sexual experiences were "firsts" that can never be relived.

4. Others were incredibly memorable and/or formative for other reasons, like the time you gave your first blowjob in the backseat of a taxi, or the time your ex made you orgasm multiple times while you hallucinated on mushrooms.

5. Worse than all the sexy stuff, maybe, you once fell for other people. Chances are, you've both had butterfly-in-the-stomach moments with former boyfriends or girlfriends and crushes that never materialized.

6. You've both experimented and gone a little wild with another special partner in crime.

7. Over the years, your partner has pined for people who rejected them outright. There's no way around it: You're dating someone else's leftovers.

8. From the time your partner was a teen, whether successful or not, they've been wooing extensively. They've spent time strategizing about how to ask someone else out and/or agonized over how to reply to flirtatious text messages you didn't send them.

9. They've likely said "I love you" to someone outside their family and friend circle who wasn't you.

10. Not to mention, envisioned building a life with that person, maybe even dreamed about what they'd name their kids together.

11. Even if you legitimately hate your exes, you both harbor precious romantic memories starring those loathsome people that your minds won't erase.

12. There's even some physical evidence of those past passions buried deep within your online presence, or in a shoebox of keepsakes tucked beneath your bed.

13. There are times when you both think about having sex with someone else—not because you're on the verge of cheating, necessarily, but because it's natural to think about other people naked.

14. As awesome as things are, you're each probably nurturing a few harmless crushes—on your personal trainer, a colleague, or a good friend of the opposite sex. You flirt with these people behind each other's backs—because it's fun, but mostly because you're human.

15. When confronted about crushing on someone else, you probably lie to each other. Because honesty can be super unkind.

16. In that vein, not every compliment you give each other is authentic. Sometimes, you tell your partner what they want or need to hear. So you might not look awesome in that hot pink halter top after all, but if your partner had been honest, you would've been late that night.

17. There will be times when you consider a life without your beloved—because you get into a terrible fight, or because you can't help considering the morbid possibility that you'll outlive them.

18. No matter how great your sex life is, not every orgasm will be mind-blowing.

19. Occasionally, you're both bound to sleep with each other out of a sense of obligation more than anything else. You'll go through the motions, faking enthusiasm while thinking about your to-do list.

20. There's no guarantee that any two people, including you and your partner, will always love each other.

21. No matter how strong your current relationship is, it will *not* always be easy. You will both fuck up. And the closer you get—the more in love you fall—the better positioned you are to hurt each other.

20

19 Signs Your Broken Relationship Is Totally Worth Saving

1. When your practical side starts reminding you that there are plenty of other fish in the proverbial sea, you instinctively tell it to shut the fuck up. You don't *want* to think about all the other great candidates out there—even the wealthier, more attractive, kinder ones. You don't want to be reassured of your market value, either. You'd rather things just went back to the way they were.

2. When you picture your significant other hooking up with someone else, it makes your stomach turn and the hair on your arms stand tall, but not out of jealousy or possessiveness. It sickens you to know you've lost something so precious—the safe, loving intimacy that once defined your coupledom—and you desperately want that back, even if you're not quite ready to do what it takes to resurrect it.

3. Being single doesn't sound awesome, even if it means you get to have sex with the guy you've been crushing on at work forever. Or that you can finally go crazy on Tindr.

4. You entertain plenty of doubts and vengeful thoughts, but once you think your hypothetical plot all the way through, you quickly realize how dumb it would be to drain the bank account, cheat, or ransack the apartment out of anger. Exacting revenge on someone you care about won't feel good.

5. You can't imagine living with anyone except your boyfriend or girlfriend. After all, your wardrobe wouldn't look quite right hanging next to anyone else's—a ridiculous thought, maybe, but whatever.

6. You can't imagine traveling with anyone but them, either. Your bras and underthings can't be packed in a suitcase with anyone else's—another ridiculous thought, maybe, but you're okay with that.

7. Lately, hanging out always seems to end in fighting, but there's no one else you'd rather waste time with. You want to binge-watch Netflix with your boyfriend or girlfriend, even if things are too contentious to risk deconstructing television plots.

8. No matter how nasty the arguments get, you still hold back the *really* nasty stuff. Something always stops you from going to the pitch-black place from which there's no turning back.

9. You still like the way your partner smells in the morning, and not just because their scent is wonderfully familiar.

10. You respect your partner as a human, even if you hate their fucking guts right now.

11. You're still physically attracted to them, too. You just don't want to have sex with them *ever* again. You'll have to, of course, eventually—when it's time to make babies. They're the only reasonable option for mothering or fathering your future children.

12. Once in a while, even now, your maddeningly obtuse partner manages to make you smile, reminding you that your inside jokes are awesomely resilient.

13. When you watch your significant other interact with strangers or acquaintances, you can't help feeling a sense of pride for being associated with them. There's value in being on the team and you know it on some level.

14. As terrible as things are, you feel automatically happy whenever your partner gets good news. No, you're not that good of a person. But your vicarious pleasure could be a sign of undying affection.

15. No bad stretch seems to blunt your ability to intuit your significant other's moods.

16. You never turn your "I'm available" light on all the way up when things get shaky.

17. It doesn't make you feel that good when strangers hit on you, anyway. If anything, being hit on reminds you how hard it is to find someone worth holding onto.

18. You know how much work it will take to get back to the good place, but the work doesn't scare you. You're willing to do whatever it takes, even if you're not quite ready to start yet.

19. You never forget the good place. When you think about your first few months as a couple, the blissful, early relationship feelings rise up from somewhere deep within to tickle your heart, reminding you that they're still there, waiting to be relit.

21

Read This If You're Feeling Betrayed By Your Boyfriend Or Girlfriend

As you grow closer as a couple, your wellbeing depends increasingly upon the choices your partner makes, both good and bad, in addition to those you make as an individual. When you navigate the world from within the context of a relationship, you're no longer alone in the cockpit, steering your own destiny—a phenomenon that's wonderfully rewarding when things go smoothly, but terribly heart wrenching when things go poorly.

Depending on the parameters of your relationship, messing up can mean a lot of different things. Every couple lives by the rules of their own unwritten (but hopefully well understood) contract. Whatever the terms, however, each person is destined to step outside the bounds of what's considered appropriate conduct on occasion. We're all fallible, after all.

Betrayals of varying degrees of significance are inevitable in a long-term relationship. If you dare to love passionately, missteps are part of the bargain. You are likely to betray—and to feel betrayed by—the person you care about most sometimes. And when this happens—when one person in a relationship fucks up royally—the fallout undoubtedly sucks for both parties. For the person who made a mistake, it sucks to feel the pangs of guilt specific to hurting someone you adore more than anyone else in the world. For the wronged party, it sucks to feel the ache of a wound so deep and painful, only someone you love madly could have cut it.

The thing is, what happens in the aftermath of a betrayal often matters more than the betrayal itself. The injured party must make a choice: They can remain bitter, or they can forgive, and move forward.

It's tempting to indulge vengeful fantasies. The desire to exact revenge—to inflict pain of equal measure on the person who elicited it in you—is entirely natural. It seems just, especially if you're in the midst of nursing an open wound. An eye for an eye, right? Wrong.

Revenge will *not* taste sweet if it means hurting your significant other—at least, it won't as long as you still genuinely love them. So if you want to salvage your bond, don't reduce yourself to your partner's level. Mimicking their misdeeds will only prolong the hurt on both ends. Other people's lapses in judgment aren't a license to act stupid or to make bad decisions. It isn't fair to invoke suffering simply because you yourself are suffering. Hurting someone deliberately is a grave crime, even—especially, maybe—in the name of payback.

Healthy romantic relationships aren't built on tit-for-tat. They're built on the courage to admit wrongdoing, and the strength to pardon one another. Behaving like a kind, respectable adult is never ill advised, no matter your partner's infraction. Set the standard. Be a good person first, and a loving boyfriend or girlfriend second. Forgive. Say "I forgive you!" out loud, when no one's around. Then say it to your significant other's face. Forgiveness is about so much more than absolving someone. It's the antidote to internal suffering, also. Those three powerful words will free you from the burden of pain, resentment, and overthinking—as long as you actually mean them.

Don't forgive anyone if you don't mean it, but don't wallow in bitterness if you don't have to, either. Forgiveness isn't easy, of course. It demands fortitude and resolve. But if you can find it in yourself to choose forgiveness, it always proves worthwhile. Embrace it as wholeheartedly and quickly as humanly possible. If you can't get there, consider ending the relationship before your spite burns it alive.

22

Read This If You're Having Doubts About Your Relationship

When you love someone madly, the last thing you expect is to entertain doubts about the strength of your bond. Questioning seems contrary to commitment. Even if you do so privately, inside your own mind—in the midst of a sleepless night, while jogging, or showering—it can feel like a serious betrayal.

After reaching a certain point, you don't want to question whether your partner's values are aligned with yours enough to move forward, long past the lustful stage and into lasting romantic attachment, or whether you want the same things out of life in practical, realistic terms, or whether you can imagine parenting together and growing old alongside each other, eventually dying hand-in-hand as you've discussed so many times while caught in the throws of passion. You don't want to let yourself ask these questions because it seems disrespectful to the person you love and the life you've built together so far.

But you must—without freaking out, if possible. Because

if you don't, those pesky questions will eat at you from the inside out until your heart is Swiss cheese, compromising your capacity to love.

No matter how strongly you feel about your significant other, it's natural to feel confused about the relationship once in a while. You might doubt the fact that the person you love loves you as much as they claim to. You might doubt that your partner is worthy of the trust you've placed in them. You might wonder if you can make it as a couple long-term. Especially in matters of the heart, none of us is all-knowing.

Pangs of uncertainty can sprout up for no good reason, tickling your consciousness and begging for attention no matter how unjustified they may be. On other occasions, your gut may respond to blatant signs of trouble, or to subtle but significant cues. Unfortunately, it's tough to know the difference. But it's always worth trying to decipher the root cause of whatever doubts creep up. You can't fear the outcome of addressing them too much to deny yourself the room to figure things out. However unpleasant the process may be, confronting uncertainty is the only way to return to a point of clarity.

You may have reason to doubt your relationship, and you may not. You may decide that the woman or man you've long thought of as "the one" is exactly right for you after all, or not. You may choose to do the work to repair whatever aspects of your relationship are broken, or deem the situation a lost cause. Relationship doubts aren't necessarily an indicator of insurmountable problems, but they can be. The morning you wake up wondering whether the person next to you belongs there, you're not doomed to split. But you might.

So listen yourself, but with the utmost caution. Don't ignore your inner voices, but don't become a victim of your own speculative thoughts, either. Be as reasonable as your emotions will allow. Seek counsel from friends and family members, but don't assume their insights are more accurate than yours. Get therapy from a trained professional, but avoid horoscopes and psychics. Cyberstalk your boyfriend, girlfriend, husband, or wife all you want, but never *ever* cybersnoop. (If you don't know the difference, figure it out.) Entertain every possibility—leaving, cheating, moving, ransacking the apartment, draining the bank account—but understand the distinction between thinking, saying, and *doing* something. Unless you're a saint who only thinks pure, saintly thoughts, don't feel obligated to express every theory or view that crosses your mind. Complete transparency isn't as healthy as it sounds, and we're all responsible to a certain extent for protecting each other from our own minds. That doesn't mean you can't communicate openly and honestly, but it does mean that you should choose your words carefully, especially when speaking to the person you love.

Ultimately, whether you have reason to be suspicious or paranoid or hesitant—whether you and your significant other stay together, or break up—you will both be fine. Love is painful and confounding and exhausting and frustrating and overwhelmingly awesome. It leads us to places we treasure, and to places we abhor. It brings out the absolute best and worst in us. Love demands navigating sharp curves, steep hills, and some impossibly giant potholes. The terrain is uneven—and that's okay. If it were simple or easy, it wouldn't be so damn hard to find, nurture, or let go of. But no one's ever died of a broken heart.

People grow apart because individuals evolve, often separately. But relationships evolve, too. If you stay together, your love will be no weaker for the questions you once pondered. On the contrary, without a doubt, you'll be stronger as a couple.

Made in the USA
Middletown, DE
12 January 2021